ALMONI

TEXT, ILLUSTRATIONS, & RECIPES

by Janet L. Doane

Seed Publishing

Friday Harbor, Washington

A Cautionary Note to the Reader

If you have questions regarding almond milk for infants or very young children, please consult with your naturopath, pediatrician, or doctor. The same applies if you suffer from gastrointestinal discomfort from eating nuts or seeds.

Seed Publishing
www.almondessence.com
ISBN: 0964951037

Dedicated

To Rex - visionary, co-creator, husband, and dear friend.

To our sons, Sam and Patrick, who have made our lives complete.

To the trees and the children of the earth.

And to Lillian - my *Almond Essence* angel.

CONTENTS

The congestive effects of dairy milk create the necessity for our family to find a healthy milk alternative. This search lasts twenty years before we discover how to make almond milk. It works with unexpected versatility in all recipes. We make the transition from dairy milk to almond milk with ease.

Follow the 4,000 year migration of almonds from China to California, and the impact that almonds have had upon countless people around the globe.

Learn about the nutrients and vital energy found in sprouted almonds and why they are good for us. Discover how inexpensive it is to make almond milk at home. Appreciate the environmental benefits that come from making almond milk. See how we stock our kitchen and cook with natural foods.

An overview of the equipment necessary for making almond milk. Simple steps to sprout almonds. Step-by-step directions to make almond milk using basic kitchen equipment. Recipes for nut and seed milk blends, almond milk kefir, seed cheese, smoothies, soup, pancakes, cereals, baked goods, hot drinks, and more.

DISCOVERY

In 1973 my husband, Rex, and I were living in Canada, when our two year old son, Sam, began to have congestive problems from pasteurized milk. He had been a breast fed baby and it took us awhile to figure out why he was having difficulties. Once identified, it wasn't long before Rex and I both noticed we were having the same problems that Sam was experiencing. This began our family's search for a healthy non-dairy milk.

Alternatives to dairy milk were limited to powdered soy milk which cost too much and provided little taste. I once spent three hours in the kitchen trying to make "delicious" soy milk from scratch using whole soybeans. After one sip, the family flatly refused to drink any more and the rest went down the kitchen drain.

In those early days of the health movement, people were just becoming aware of lactose intolerance and the congestive effects of dairy products. Usage of hormones and antibiotics to boost dairy production were completely unheard of by the public. We learned of the advantages of drinking raw, unpasteurized milk, and upon finding certified dairy milk at the health food store, made the switch. The congestive problems diminished dramatically, undoubtedly due to the enzymes present in the raw milk that enabled us to digest it properly.

Yet despite the benefits, a subtle, persistent feeling would often come to mind: this milk was produced by cows for

the nursing of *their* babies - and they
have four stomachs! Was it safe
enough to drink unpasteurized? I couldn't help
wondering if there
wasn't another kind
of milk - one that was
healthful for us (and
especially for a child);
was simple and
inexpensive to make;
one that tasted delicious and
would help us become less
dependent upon animals for food.

In 1976 baby Patrick (also breast fed) arrived. A shift in
Rex's job relocated us to southern California, haven for
alternative life-styles. With the baby and five year old
Sam, we began settling in and making new friends, who
were soon invited for dinner. They were vegetarians and
advocates of a raw, living food diet, something we knew
little about. Upon asking them what they would like to
eat, they suggested fresh fruit and fruit smoothies made
with nut milk. When I inquired on how I might make
such a drink, they said, "Oh, just put some nuts and
fruits into the blender with water and blend on high
speed for awhile". It sounded simple enough.

Not knowing which nuts or seeds to use, or that certain
blending techniques would create a better textured
smoothie, I filled the blender with raw sunflower seeds,

7

bananas, dates and water, and set the machine whirring. The result was a smoothie that was anything but smooth. It was thick with lumps of sunflower pulp, and tasted overly sweet *and* oddly bitter. Fortunately our guests didn't complain - perhaps they were just being polite. It didn't occur to me at the time to try different nuts, such as almonds.

Although healthful, this first smoothie lacked some essential qualities - a smooth texture and a pleasing taste. We wanted a nut milk that could mix well with fruits for smoothies, and have the right properties to use with recipes for baking - and the sunflower seed milk was definitely not the answer.

Despite our first disasters with making nut milk, Rex and I remained intrigued by its potential. Over the next twenty years we would occasionally try again, still hoping to succeed, but would be disappointed because of the amount of pulp, or a taste that we didn't like.

Our first exciting breakthrough came when we found Ann Wigmore's basic almond milk recipe in her book, *The Sprouting Book*. It was the best nut milk we'd tasted. We took Ms. Wigmore's recipe to heart and began experimenting. After a few weeks (and a lot of mess!) of working with the proportions of the ingredients and various blending techniques, we began to make a very satisfying milk in less than five minutes per batch! Our frustrations from the past had finally been transformed, as we whipped up quarts of delicious, energizing, almond milk anytime we wanted.

We got hooked on a morning banana smoothie (page 53). We just couldn't seem to start the day without one - and even now, so many years later, this recipe remains a real favorite.

Baking followed fast on the heels of our smoothie triumph. We were delighted to discover that muffins, biscuits, and quick breads cooked as well with almond milk as they had with dairy milk. Grains such as rice and quinoa became richer when cooked with a little almond milk. Later we tried almond milk in soups such as Butternut Bisque (page 71) and in sauces for rice, or veggie patties (page 75). As you might guess, almond milk passed each test with flying colors.

Yet even with how good almond milk tasted, and how easy it was to cook with, making a complete change took time. For months we made "half and half" - a blend of 50% almond milk and 50% dairy milk that we used in coffee, or with cold breakfast cereals. After many more months, the percentage became 100% almond milk.

A year passed, and we rarely used the weekly quart of dairy milk we were still purchasing "just in case". Even our morning cup of coffee - which seemed impossible to even *consider* having without dairy milk - eventually gave way.

Over time we added more healthful hot drinks made from nourishing carob powder, spicy teas, or organic cocoa. As we sipped from steaming, richly flavored beverages laced with sweet almond milk and a little honey, we hardly ever missed those freshly ground Kona beans. Well, almost never...

Often during our morning "cocoa talks", we marveled at the natural process that had taken place. We hadn't wanted to force the change, or to impose a strict regimen away from dairy. It made sense that if almond milk was right for us, the intrinsic knowledge held within our bodies would make the change. We watched it all happen and experienced it, allowing ourselves go off of dairy over a period of time. And the transformation has lasted.

Looking back I can see that we were lucky in that our babies weren't in need of a milk substitute or formula. They were both nursed for over a year, yet I wish we had known about sprouted almond milk - I think they would have loved it.

Currently there is debate about how early an infant can have almond, rice, oat, and soy milk. Some of the information on soy milk (because of soy's phytoestrogens) is disturbing because of its effect on the body's hormones. We have found a lot of information from searching the internet to familiarize ourselves with this subject, and recommend anyone seeking advice to do so in order to learn what questions are important to ask.

Most almond milk studies have not, to my knowledge, been done with sprouted almonds. Sprouting changes the chemistry of the almond by neutralizing the enzyme inhibitors.

One important study has been done with lipase, present

in almonds, which is the enzyme that *digests fats*.

If the almonds are not sprouted, this enzyme cannot be utilized by our bodies because of the enzyme inhibitors in the nuts that keep the lipase bound. But once sprouted (soaked), the lipase becomes bio-available, along with many other beneficial enzymes, essential fatty acids, and carbohydrates that have changed into natural sugars. All this adds up to a balanced "living food".

Keep in mind that homemade almond milk is a food that is not commercially prepared. It's "alive", and will probably have small variations in each batch. Even still, we have found it well worth the effort to make because of the special culinary and nutritional qualities found in sprouted almond milk.

Roots

The roots of almonds run deep, extending far across the world, into the distant past. A taste of the sweet nut hardly reveals the story of its enduring origins, colorful history, and path traveled to reach the central valley of California, the land destined to become the heart of almond country.

In doing research for this book, Rex and I were fascinated to learn how ancient this nut-producing tree is. Millions of years ago, as massive geological forces gave shape to the Himalayan Mountains, the wild almond tree, *Prunus communis* (ancestor of today's cultivars), grew in the arid steppes and deserts of southwestern Asia, in southern Russia, and in China. Hardy stands of this tree still bear fruit in limited areas of the Kopet-Dagh and Tian Shan Mountains, which border northeastern India and Russia. How almonds traveled from those rugged regions to the Mediterranean area, and onward to the Americas is a vivid story, because it appears that wherever explorers, travelers, trading merchants, and conquerors have gone, so too have almonds.

As the pages of almonds' history turned, it was easy to imagine a world several thousand years ago. Visions sprang to life of hearty breeds of people, some being the adventurous merchant-traders who trekked the Silk Road, the main trading route from China to the Middle East. The merchants bought and sold unique treasures of silks, precious stones, foods and spices, and shared ideas of medicine, religion, philosophy, and science with people of similar interests. This route was utilized for over 1,500 years and became the foundation for the spread of almonds throughout the vast geographic area.

Scholars tell us the earliest caravans consisted of a hundred or more people. They traversed through geographically hostile regions of deserts, steppes, and mountains as they made the grueling 12,000 mile round trip - a journey that took eight or nine years to complete! Imagine.... several of these trips could define a person's whole lifetime.

Wild stands of almond trees grew in some of these regions, and the almonds were undoubtedly harvested in the early fall, stored in saddle bags, or pressed to obtain the highly prized oil. This provided portable and nutritious foods to sustain the travelers throughout their arduous expeditions.

Cultivation occurred in an organic way. Travelers touted the benefits of almonds as they circulated from village to village. Seeds planted along the Silk Road eventually spread to reach the Mediterranean Sea. Here, ingenious Phoenecian traders furthered the proliferation of almonds as they navigated the 2,000 mile waterway, introducing and educating the peoples of bordering countries to the versatile nut.

Around this same time, the people of Judea tasted the delicious "sheked", the Hebrew word for almond. A person walking past a neighboring farm may have had a conversation with the owner of the land who mentioned that the "sheked" trees had been producing a sweet, good nut, and that his wife used them frequently in cooking. One of their favorite breads had ground almonds pressed into the tops of the loaves before baking. And he was planning to plant more seeds after the rains had soaked the ground. Some would sprout and grow into nut-bearing trees, helping to maintain their food supply over the coming years.

Two millennia later, Roman soldiers on their tour of duty huddled around an evening fire, sharing a handful of almonds as part of their meal. If placed in slow burning embers the nuts would have roasted to perfection, making a delicious, warm treat. The soldiers' crusades and expeditions pushed almonds further afield, and soon Roman farmers were cultivating trees throughout the Empire, from as far as Egypt to England.

When the Moorish armies swept through 7th century Spain, they brought not only their customs, culture, religious beliefs, and architecture, but almonds, or "lous", as well. Women dressed in shawls and long dresses may have been seen in their kitchens, bending over a sturdy wooden table crushing nuts with a mortar and pestle. The pulverized almonds were then stirred into soups, or sprinkled over fish that baked with sprigs of fresh rosemary in open hearth ovens.

Common everyday events such as these were enacted in countless versions over thousands of years: people ate almonds in every possible way - fresh from the shell, simmered in soups, served with roasted meats, fish, or vegetables, ground and baked in breads, added to cooked cereals or rice, and occasionally used whole in hot drinks, or as garnishes. The versatility of the nut was inexhaustible, and its sweet flavor was compatible with almost every conceivable dish. This made almonds highly valued in every culture and country where they grew.

The forces that had pushed almonds upon these lands rested quietly for nearly a thousand years until the 1600's when shifts in awareness whetted man's appetite for discovering new frontiers. The point of departure would be Spain, and the men, "conquistadores", the fierce conqueror-explorers. They forged their way across the waters of the Atlantic Ocean, sailing to the New World in search of gold. In the bellies of the ships, almonds and enough other food to last for months were stored. Perhaps one such captain paced the wooden decks in his finely crafted leather boots, and dreamed of the wealth and fame he would claim for himself and his country. What he didn't realize was the important role he was playing in bringing almonds to the Americas. His imagination would have been staggered had he foreseen the amount of money that the sale of almonds would generate centuries later as a cash crop.

A hundred years after the conquistadores conquered Mexico, the Franciscan padres arrived in what is now California. Wearing loosely belted robes, and carrying few possessions, they rode and walked with their donkeys or horses up and down an earthen, coastal road that came to be known as El Camino Real - The Royal Road.

It was a lengthy stretch covering some 500 miles - from San Diego in the south, to Sonoma - fifty miles north of San Francisco. As they tended to their missionary work they planted almond trees around their adobe missions, and along El Camino Real.

The destiny of almonds would eventually find fulfillment in the fertile inland valleys where the Padres sowed the first seeds. Trees planted along the coast had borne few nuts, partly due to weather that was too cool and moist - yet the flowers made a beautiful display in the spring. It would take the wisdom of horticulturists who came a century later who understood the importance of cross-pollination to bring the trees to their full potential.

The practice of cross-pollination, plus the more inland climate of the Sacramento Valley, provided nearly perfect growing conditions (much like the Mediterranean's) for almond trees to flourish. The horticulturists' early cultivars produced abundant crops - varieties of almonds that remain in high demand today.

The first cooperative dedicated solely to growing and selling almonds was established in 1920. The business blossomed to its present size of 7,000 growers who farm 400,000 acres in the Sacramento and San Joaquin valleys of central California. This fertile stretch produces a harvest of *500 million tons of almonds annually*, supplying almost the entire United States market! In addition, California almonds are exported to eighty-eight countries around the world, thereby symbolically completing

17

the immense circle of their western migration.

The future of the almond is uniquely linked with our own... so keeping this in mind, pop one into your mouth, bite deep, and savor the taste of history.

NATURE'S BOUNTY

On a trip to Modesto in the northernmost edge of the almond producing region, Rex and I visited the Almond Board of California to gather information for this book. Our timing couldn't have been better, for spring was under way, and thousands of acres of almond trees were in full bloom. We were hoping to have an opportunity to actually see, touch, and walk the land that produces this extraordinary nut.

After an encouraging visit at the Board, we headed by car toward the groves, exiting the freeway onto a small farm road. The orchards that came into view dazzled us visually, for they looked like a fairyland of trees. Stopping the car to get out, we breathed deeply and were nearly overtaken by the heady, sweet perfume from the almond flowers.

The panorama was classically Californian. Wide open hills, turned emerald green from winter rains, were framed by distant coastal mountains. Everything the eye could see rested under the bluest sky. Sunlight danced off thousands of tiny, pinkish-white blossoms, stunningly backlit against the black-brown branches of the trees. Soft breezes carried the flowers pungent fragrance, and bees were everywhere gathering pollen (in what seemed to be a smorgasbord of gargantuan proportion), ensuring a good crop.

Standing on the fertile soil of that small grove, I contemplated the 4,000 years it had taken to bring almonds to America, as well as the immense power inherent in the cycles of life, renewal, and giving. I knew our future food was connected to the almond trees. In previous seasons the annual harvests had produced *ten billion pounds* of nuts from the almond country's 400,000 acres, thereby feeding countless people, much like me, throughout the world.

THE ESSENCE OF AN ALMOND

The beauty of that region reflects the outstanding nut it produces. Almonds belong to the most nutritionally concentrated type of food - seeds - and have the best ratio of important nutrients to calories of any nut, being exceptionally high in Vitamin E, essential for keeping the heart strong. And because almonds are a plant food, they contain no cholesterol.

In eating these tasty nuts we treat ourselves to high quality plant protein, fiber, significant amounts of iron, calcium, magnesium, phosphorus, potassium, zinc, folic acid, selenium, copper, quercitin, and B vitamins. In addition, almonds are loaded with phytochemicals - biologically active, beneficial plant compounds that scientists have discovered help in preventing cancer, osteoporosis, and in lowering high levels of cholesterol.

VITAMIN E AND YOUR HEART

Dr. Gary Fraser, cardiologist with Loma Linda University, conducted a six year study with 26,000 Seventh Day Adventists (who typically follow a vegetarian diet). The results of his research not only challenged the common belief that nuts are to be avoided (because of the fat), but demonstrated they can be eaten freely, enhancing our health considerably. His findings showed that people who ate a small handful of almonds five times a week reduced their rate of possible heart attack or coronary death by 50%, compared to those who did not!

FATS, EFA'S, FAT GRAMS

As for the fat content, let's take a look. We know that saturated fats, trans-fats, and margarine can cause health problems. Recently, many scientific studies have been conducted that prove there are many kinds of fats that are good for us - in fact, they are essential for maintaining health.

Mono-unsaturated fat (in almonds) can help control and even lower serum cholesterol. In contrast, pasteurized dairy milk is 60% *saturated* fat and cholesterol *forming*.

A well balanced Omega essential fatty acid (EFA) "cocktail"

21

can be made from a variety of nuts and seeds. Each nut or seed has concentrations of Omega 3, 6, or 9. For example, hemp, flax, and chia seeds (and their oils), may be among the best sources of Omega 3's for vegetarians, the type that most of us often need.

Quality cold pressed oils are also sources for a range of EFA's. Look for almond, grapeseed (outstanding for cooking because it has a high heat tolerance), walnut, avocado, sesame, coconut, borage, flax, and pumpkin seed oils. Keep all oils in a cool dark place. Flax oil must be refrigerated as it can become rancid. I prefer to grind the seeds before each use to make sure the oils are completely fresh.

I've recently learned about immune enhancing coconut oil with its antiviral, antifungal, and antibacterial properties. The oil is also known for assisting weight loss because it increases the body's metabolism, and helps to balance the thyroid gland.

In almonds, research has shown that lipase, the fat digesting enzyme, is available to humans *only when almonds are sprouted*. When not sprouted, the lipase cannot do its job because of the enzyme inhibitors present in the nuts. These inhibitors are nature's way to make sure nuts and seeds do not sprout until they are in favorable growing conditions. When we sprout nuts and seeds ourselves, this converts and neutralizes the enzyme inhibitors and all the goodness is unlocked for our benefit.

One cup of almond milk has only 90 calories, compared to 160 calories for whole dairy milk. Both have similar amounts of fat - 7 grams for almond milk, and 9 grams for dairy milk. A smoothie made with one half cup of almond milk contains 3 $\frac{1}{2}$ fat grams and 45 calories, plus the calories from the addition of fruit.

WHY FRESH IS SO GOOD FOR US

When I sprout (soak) almonds for 10 - 12 hours, a simple process that takes only minutes of actual time (page 38) the health benefits dramatically increase. The activated enzymes convert fats into essential fatty acids, starches into simple sugars, and complex proteins into amino acids, the building blocks of protein. What this means to me is that my body is able to utilize sprouted almond milk with ease, receiving an abundance of fresh, lively nutrients.

This is one reason that making milk from sprouted almonds is a welcome addition to the diet. Since cooking is unnecessary, all the almonds' vital properties are preserved - especially the enzymes - those mysterious elements that build life and energy, and keep us young. Foods of this high quality can help to balance the effects of eating processed foods.

The protein content (2+ grams per cup, equal to mothers milk) and easy digestibility make it a great choice for people with sensitive digestion. If you, like the members of our family, have reactions to dairy milk, almond milk can provide comforting relief.

If there is uncertainty about hormones or antibiotics that may be present in cow's milk, almond milk offers a holistic alternative. We especially love the fact that the freshness date is never a concern, simply because we make almond milk every couple of days. And for anyone concerned with animal rights issues, almond milk provides a cruelty-free food that can be completely enjoyed with every meal.

COSTS

Surprisingly, the cost of almond milk is often *less* than dairy milk. Almond prices can vary over the year, depending on crop yields, and where you shop. Currently, the price for a pound of almonds runs between $3.00 - $9.00. This may seem expensive at first glance, but it breaks down into affordable quarts of milk using the basic recipe of 1/2 cup of almonds blended with 4 cups water.

When I pour out a pound of dry almonds into a measuring container, it comes to 3 cups. This is enough to make 6 quarts of milk. Divide 6 into the price per pound, and the cost for each quart will be found.

Given the above prices, the cost will fall between 50 cents to $1.50 per quart! This is much less than what I would pay for ready-made dairy-free products that have flooded the supermarkets and health food stores.

Health food stores often offer discounts for bulk purchases - so if almond milk becomes a staple food like it has for us, buying in bulk makes good sense. We get unsprayed almonds and other nuts and seeds mail-order from Azure Standard (page 103) and the prices and quality are excellent.

GOOD FOR THE PLANET

Almonds come from trees, nature's own renewable food resource. The trees provide more than just nuts to eat - the orchards create beneficial ecosystems for birds and bees (and more), with extensive roots that help to prevent soil erosion. Beauty, oxygen, and nuts are just a few precious gifts that come from the almond trees.

When I make almond milk, the need for throwaway milk containers or packaging is eliminated. This in turn helps reduce the distressing amount of waste products that are dumped into our landfills. Wise use of our land is one vital way to preserve a healthy future for our children.

Sometimes I think I'm not doing enough to help with the ecology, but then remember that each and every conscious act I make for the good of the whole - even seemingly insignificant ones - combine with the millions of other positive choices that countless other people are making every day. And it all adds up to make a difference.

OUR NATURAL FOODS KITCHEN

As a prelude to the recipes that follow, we invite you to take a peek into our kitchen to see how we are set up to cook with natural foods. Part of this involves what I call "intuitive eating", listening to the body's wisdom regarding what is best to eat. Often, there is a difference between what might *taste good*, versus what the deeper nutritional needs of the body may be.

The recipes in this book will support a decision or necessity to transition off dairy, wheat, eggs, and sugar, or for learning how to incorporate more raw food into the diet. We became vegetarians in 1969, then vegan in 1995, and now like to eat mostly uncooked food to flood the body with enzymes and life energy. (The index has links for information on vegan, vegetarian, and raw food.)

It is interesting to note that Rex's and my perceptions of food - of what actually tastes good to us - has changed over time. A colorful salad and seed cheese (page 60) can seem like a feast, whereas years earlier we might have felt deprived. Now, a couple times a year, a bite or two of dessert when we eat out with friends is more than enough to satisfy our desire for those comfort foods.

I'm fortunate in that I love to prepare meals. My mother says that our kitchen smells like "a real country kitchen", undoubtedly from all the fruits ripening in large bowls. I find the fruits' bright colors, beautiful shapes, and enticing fragrances a constant source of inspiration.

We keep a wide array of produce, plus many herbs and spices on hand to create savory meals. We discovered that grapeseed oil is the best for cooking, because it can tolerate higher heat without degrading into a trans-fat. It is so very light and delicate in taste which makes it perfect for salads and veggies. Other oils (olive, walnut, sesame) are still enjoyed, usually drizzled over the food at the table.

The refrigerator is packed with fresh vegetables - just ask our friends! We store everything from apples to zucchini, maple syrup, soy-free miso, hot Thai curry paste, mustard, homemade raw pickles, and vinegars. Plus there are always almonds and sunflower seeds that have been soaked, ready for use, and a container of almond milk (page 40), and some almond milk kefir (page 50).

The right kitchen utensils contribute to the pleasure of preparing meals. Our Krups model 239 blender is one of the most frequently used machines for making almond milk, smoothies, seed cheese, and more. A good blender can also grind whole grains for making the *freshest*, best tasting hot cereal and flour for cookies and muffins. (**Note:** See section on blenders and equipment, page 33.)

There's a powerful Champion juicer for extracting fresh juices from fruits and vegetables, and a "Little Pro Plus" Cuisinart that saves time with chopping or grating vegetables, and with making pesto. Our pots and pans are Lifetime (a special line from Westbend), heavy duty stainless steel, and true to their name, have lasted for over thirty years and are still going strong.

It takes some planning to have this much food on hand, but this is what enables us to prepare just about any meal we might want. Since Rex and I both work at home, eating in saves a considerable amount of money. Our schedule is flexible which allows us the freedom to shop for food as needed. Without spending so much money on packaged foods, we can put the amount saved into buying organic produce. (If the organic produce is wilted or old, we buy conventional varieties, because the life energy in food is equally important to us.)

When we're hungry we select foods that look enticing or sound good, like banana smoothie (page 53), or Ruby Red Purifying Salad (page 68). Sometimes we follow a recipe, but more often use it as a general guide. We improvise with what's on hand, making food that satisfies our needs and the mood of the moment. In this way we often discover a new dish.

We enjoy our local farmers market that runs from May to October in this northern climate. Weekly trips boost our appreciation for the effort involved in growing food, and fosters relationships with the farmers whose organic fruits, vegetables, and flowers, bring us so much energy and joy. We like to buy heirloom varieties, knowing that this supports the healthy practice of plant diversity and helps to keep the giant agri-businesses from taking over.

After coming home from the market I like to fill the kitchen sink with cold water and soak all the produce with a tablespoon of food grade hydrogen peroxide for 10 - 15 minutes. This removes unwanted contaminants and bugs, and the produce stays fresh longer.

CONCLUSION

After ten years of drinking almond milk it continues to play an integral role in our daily life. I would try making anything with almond milk, it remains so versatile, delicious, and easy to cook with!

Remember that almond milk is *made at home*, so it will have "personality". Learn how the milk-making process works for you. The instructions in this book are a way to begin - but if you discover other techniques, all the better! A friend of mine once said she started with my directions, but then found her own easy rhythm.

Rex reminds me that life is a continuing artform. Having a good time while preparing meals, giving thanks for the bounty in our lives, creates a sense of well being and happiness that continues to grow with each year.

Recipes & How-To's

*Vegetarian, vegan, and raw
food recipes made without
dairy, sugar, or eggs.*

Transforming Nuts Into Milk

Nut Milk Blends

Recipes Using Almond Milk & Milk Blends

TRANSFORMING NUTS INTO MILK

A note to parents with infants: *Occasionally I receive email from mothers wondering if sprouted almond milk is okay to give to their infants. I am not a certified health practitioner, and as such, am not qualified to advise. If you have any concerns, please consult with your pediatrician, naturopath, or doctor. Likewise, do the same if you have trouble digesting nuts.*

THE PROCESS OF MAKING SPROUTED ALMONDS INTO MILK

All the information I know about how to make the most delicious almond milk is here. Once each person finds his or her own rhythm, almond milk can be made in minutes and enjoyed throughout a lifetime!

Whenever I begin something new there is always a learning curve - a time when things feel awkward. This was equally true with learning how to make sprouted almond milk - it took a lot of time to figure it all out.

Almond milk is a *handmade food*, subject to fluctuations. It doesn't come in a bottle or a box. The milk is not made with huge machines, filled with additives or binders, nor is it homogenized and pasteurized so that it will always be the same. Almond milk is a *living food*, and like most of us, some days are better than others.

Making almond milk at home is a bit like making pancakes - the first batch doesn't always come out just right. In the Discovery chapter (pages 6 - 11) I share how many attempts we made at making almond milk until we found a good recipe. Even after many years I *still* encounter variations. These small quirks are offset by the knowledge that I am taking the time to make something of value, something that will feed and nourish my body and those whom I love.

I think this milk is delicious, especially when made with sprouted almonds, vanilla, and a few cashews. People often have wonderful responses when they hear about almond milk, and on tasting it (especially the smoothie recipes), often oooh and ahhh with surprise because they didn't think it would taste so good!

THE IMPORTANCE OF EQUIPMENT

FINDING A GREAT BLENDER

One of the most important aspects for success in making almond milk is finding the right equipment.

For starters, blenders with a powerful motor with wattage anywhere between 350 to 500 are usually good - look on the bottom of the blender base. Also, blenders tops that are shaped like a "V" force whatever is being blended to be pushed down to where the blades are.

Both of these factors - a powerful motor and a "V" shaped top - will provide a better textured milk - in short, less pulp.

We have known people who didn't have good blenders who made almond milk and there was far too much pulp to drink plain. The milk was best used for baking and making smoothies, and at least they could stop using dairy milk for some recipes.

However, blenders that are not powerful can be used to pre-grind nuts or seeds to use in conjunction with a Soy Quick *machine* (see below). This actually helps the Soy Quick to make a much better milk. A food processor will also work to pre-grind.

The **Soy Quick** is even quieter than our Krups. It has a built in strainer - a stainless steel caddy with hundreds of tiny perforations that holds the nuts. The blades fit into this caddy through an ingenious design. As the machine whirs, the liquids pass through the caddy's perforations, but the pulp stays inside.

At first, the biggest drawback was that a lot of slivered almonds and a considerable amount of pulp remained in the caddy after blending - way more than if I had made the milk in a blender.

Then I discovered if I pre-ground the almonds and other nuts or seeds with a little water in the blender, and poured this mixture through the hopper that feeds directly into the Soy Quick's caddy, I would get an excellent quality milk with far less pulp.

The results from the Soy Quick are consistent and the finished milk is excellent for drinking plain. The machine also has an optional heating element, so the milk can be warmed - even cooked if necessary.

When our trusty Krups, model 239, was wearing out we bought another brand on e-Bay that was listed for a great price. (We didn't think we could get the Krups model anymore, but later discovered that the 239 could still be found on e-Bay and bought one.)

We'd used the other brand before (but a different model) and although louder and not quite as strong as the Krups, we felt we could make do with it for awhile. The model we bought was so incredibly noisy (even without anything in it) that I literally ran out of the kitchen with both hands covering my ears, and felt jarred for hours.

Rex and I had ringing in the ears afterward. We delegated the machine to the trash - I didn't even want to give it to the local thrift shop and submit someone else to the same abuse. Later we read some reviews about that same model with similar complaints... live and learn. Perhaps I should have sent the blender back to the company with a letter of explanation - that might have done some good.

So... do homework! If you are in a store, and if it's possible, ask to plug in the display blender you are considering buying to actually listen to the sound of the motor. It will be obvious if it's going to be noisy or not. Remember that **glass tops are much quieter** than plastic ones, and will look nice for years.

The internet can help, but often the reviews for the same brand or model will say "it's fantastic", or "it's terrible".

This can be exasperating.

If your blender is loud, please make sure to **take precautions to protect the tender ears of babies and little children, as well as your own hearing**. A kitchen towel wrapped around the blender's motor base and another at the bottom of the glass top can help to muffle the sound and protect from long-term exposure to high decibel levels.

If your blender is intolerably loud, another option is to wear earplugs, leave the room, or buy a new machine!

STRAINERS

The right size strainer will facilitate making almond milk. A regular 5" diameter, fine-mesh strainer from the grocery store or kitchen shop works best. Stainless steel mesh, rather than plastic, will last the longest. Strainers with ultra-fine mesh (tea strainers) collect too much pulp, while those with large-size mesh (for draining pasta) collect none.

ABOUT SPROUTED ALMONDS

It's easy to sprout almonds. In just 10 - 12 hours the goodness locked inside the kernel changes into a growing, living food. Sprouted almonds are moister, softer to chew, and easier to digest. They taste so much sweeter and lose that strong "almondy" flavor. The sweetness is a definite plus!

Sprouting enlivens the enzymes that are dormant within each almond. These enzymes activate when they come in contact with water (the soaking process), and the nuts are "awakened". The potential growth for each almond is to become a tree - and when we eat sprouted almonds our bodies receive this concentrated vital energy and nutrition (page 20).

If I run out of sprouted almonds, that's okay - unsprouted almonds are nutritious too. There are times when we make milk this way, having forgotten to start the sprouting process the day before, or because we've used up all the available milk. But I try to make sure that most of the time the almonds are soaked. One good reason is that **the fat digesting enzyme, lipase, is available to humans only when the almonds have sprouted.** Otherwise this enzyme remains dormant because of the almonds' own enzyme inhibitors that change only when

37

conditions become favorable for its growth (soaking). This is why seeds can still sprout after hundreds of years.

THE TASTE OF ALMOND MILK

Sprouted almond milk has a natural sweetness and a delicate flavor that stands on its own. Adding a few cashews creates a creamier milk with more "body" that can be used with every dish. Adding vanilla is like "icing on the cake", and honey is not necessary at all.

Unsprouted almond milk has a stronger almondy flavor, much like eating raw almonds. This is why honey and vanilla are in the recipe - to add sweetness and flavor.

STEPS TO SPROUT ALMONDS

Use only raw, whole, unpeeled almonds. I start soaking

either in the morning, or the night before. Check the almonds and remove any that are broken - these can be used in other recipes.

1. Put 1/2 cup almonds in a wide mouth glass jar or ceramic container.

2. Cover with two cups of pure, cold water.

3. Place anywhere in the kitchen *away from direct sunlight* to keep from overheating the water. Almonds do not need light to sprout, only normal room temperatures. Soak for about 10 - 12 hours.

I like to rinse the almonds after they have soaked for several hours, then cover again with fresh water and continue the process.

4. After soaking for 10 - 12 hours, pour the water off the almonds (or directly through a strainer) and rinse with cold water. Don't be surprised that the water is brown. This comes from the cinnamon colored skins. Drain.

5. Keep the almonds in the glass jar and cover with a lid. Or, if using a strainer, slip it inside a clean zip lock bag to hold in the moisture. Refrigerate. Leave the almonds in the jar, or wrapped, until you are ready to use them. The almonds will become even sweeter and moister in another day.

Stored this way, almonds will stay fresh for 4 - 5 days. If at any time they develop an odor, taste bitter, or look mildewed, throw them out and start another batch.

Remember to rinse and drain the almonds each day.

HOW TO MAKE ALMOND MILK

1/2 cup sprouted almonds

1/2 teaspoon vanilla extract

2 teaspoons honey (if almonds are unsprouted)

4 cups pure cold water

BLENDING PROCESS

1. For sprouted almonds: rinse briefly, drain, and place in a clean, dry blender.

2. For unsprouted almonds: place in a clean, dry blender, and pulse until as powdery as possible.

**3. *Just cover* with water (1/2 inch). Pulse to break up sprouted almonds into small pieces.

4. Start on low speed and go to high speed for 1 minute.

5. Turn blender off.

6. Add 1/2 cup more water, vanilla, and optional honey.

7. Start on low speed and go to highest speed for another minute. (If the milk seems too thick, add tiny amounts of water. The consistency should be like thick cream.)

8. Turn blender off.

9. Add the rest of the water and pulse to mix.

10. Turn blender off.

11. Strain.

Pour the milk through a strainer into a serving container and refrigerate. **Tip:** If I jiggle the strainer or tap it against the blender as I pour, the milk keeps flowing. Press the last bit of pulp with a spoon for every drop of
milk. It will stay fresh for 2 - 3 days. Almond milk can be frozen - eight cubes equals about 1/2 cup.

The strainer will catch anywhere from 1 - 2 tablespoons (or less) of pulp from the almonds (mostly skins) that can't be blended. For some reason, sprouted almonds have more pulp. Some people put the pulp into loaves, breads, or hot cereal. Sometimes we give the pulp to the birds, the "little guys" - the Juncos - and they seem to love it.

Why is there pulp? Because we are using blenders that are still a bit inefficient for this process. Someday, someone will invent a powerful, affordable machine that will eliminate the problems discussed here - but until that time comes we are making good use of what is readily available.

Too much pulp? This is the most common experience. If

I have more than a couple tablespoons of pulp, which still happens on occasion, I might have started with too much water. I put the pulp back into the blender with about 1/2 cup of water and **blend again** on the highest speed for about 60 seconds, then strain.

SETTLING

Remember this is a homemade food, so even though it's been strained, the milk will have some texture (unless you're using the Soy Quick machine described on page 34). Some people like the texture, others don't.

The liquids and solids tend to separate after straining. *To drink the milk plain, let it settle for about 30 minutes* because some of the pulp the strainer doesn't catch floats to the surface of the milk before settling to the bottom of the container. If the pulp is bothersome, swish a tea strainer across the top of the milk to remove particles, then put the pulp back into the container for later use.

Sometimes I add another cup of water when I reach the "dregs" of the container, and it stretches the milk for one more smoothie, or cup of cocoa.

And now, energizing almond milk is ready to use!

USES FOR EXTRA ALMOND MILK & SPROUTED ALMONDS

* Eat sprouted almonds as a snack. The skins can be peeled off quite easily.

* Sprouted whole almonds make a tasty topping for salads such as Ruby Red Purifying Salad (page 68).

* Grind sprouted almonds in a food processor or blender to put on top of fresh fruit or hot cereal.

* Add sprouted almonds when making pesto (page 65).

* Freeze extra almond milk in ice cube trays. Eight cubes equals about 1/2 cup of milk. Store in tightly covered freezer containers or bags.

* Use extra milk to make kefir (page 50).

* Use sprouted almonds to make raw food cookies (page 78).

* Keep the blender clean for the most hygienic milk.

NUT MILK BLENDS

Almonds combine deliciously with other nuts and seeds. This can help to create a balance of Omega 3, 6, and 9 essential fatty acids (EFA's) from the foods we eat.

Rex and I enjoy making a number of milk blends with subtle flavors. Almonds contain Omega 6 EFA, and have many healthy nutrients, such as Vitamin E, quercitin, and phytochemicals - beneficial plant compounds that help prevent cancer and osteoporosis. (See pages 20 - 25.)

Flax, chia, and hemp seeds are all excellent sources of Omega 3's from vegetal sources. Research has shown that Omega 3 is the EFA that many of us are deficient in. The ratio of EFA 3, to 6 and 9, in hemp, flax, and chia seeds are the right balance for maintaining body health, so it's good to include these seeds with almond milk. Rex and I have been impressed at how much better we have felt since including them in our diet.

When I make almond milk blends I don't increase the water in the basic recipe (page 40). The extra nuts or seeds give the milk a little more "body", which I like. I've included the almond-date milk recipe here because it is so delicious and can be used as a base milk for other ingredients.

ALMOND-DATE MILK

High energy, potassium-rich dates make a delicious addition to almond milk. Delete the honey from the basic almond milk recipe because the dates have so much sweetness.

Soak 3 - 4 Medjool dates for several hours. Remove seeds, cut into small pieces. Add to previously made almond milk, or, when starting a fresh batch (page 40). Blend on highest speed until thoroughly mixed. Strain.

ALMOND - CASHEW MILK

This is our "workhorse recipe" which we use almost all the time. Cashews add creaminess and sweetness that is particularly good with hot drinks, or *any* recipe, for that matter.

Add 2 - 3 tablespoons of raw cashews to the almond milk basic recipe (page 40) and proceed as directed.

ALMOND - PUMPKIN SEED MILK

Pumpkin seeds are high in zinc, a trace mineral that is often hard to find. Zinc helps to maintain a healthy immune system. The taste of sprouted pumpkin seeds is light and mellow - but if not sprouted the flavor is "smokier", and stronger. (Recipe continues.)

Soak 2 tablespoons of pumpkin seeds in the same jar with the almonds (page 38), and then follow the directions for the basic almond milk recipe (page 40). I often include some cashews with this mix too.

ALMOND - TAHINI MILK

Tahini, a golden colored seed butter made from roasted, finely ground sesame seeds, is high in calcium. For recipes that call for a nutty, slightly peanut-buttery taste, such as cookies or sauces with Middle Eastern flavors, try this blend.

Add 1 - 2 tablespoons of tahini to almond milk. Blend. You can also grind 2 tablespoons hulled, raw sesame seeds in a coffee mill or blender for a raw version, and add to the basic almond milk recipe (page 40).

ALMOND - HEMP SEED - CASHEW MILK

Raw, organic hemp seeds are very high in Omega 3 EFA, protein, chlorophyll, all eight amino acids, and gamma linoleic acid - GLA - which, like Evening Primrose oil, helps to maintain hormonal balance. Rex and I have experienced many health benefits since incorporating hemp seeds and hemp seed oil into our diet.

2 tablespoons raw hemp seeds
2 tablespoons raw cashews

Add the seeds and nuts to the basic almond milk recipe (page 40). Or put seeds into smoothies and blend well.

ALMOND - OAT MILK

High energy, strengthening oats, create a more substantial milk. This is a yummy milk for making kefir (page 50).

2 tablespoons uncooked quick, or baby oats
2 cups pure water
1/16 teaspoon sea salt
1 1/2 cups almond milk (page 40)

Pulse oats and salt in a dry blender or coffee mill until powdery. Pour water into pan. Heat over medium flame. Add oat flour, stirring, and bring to a simmer. Stir until oats thicken, 2 - 3 minutes. Turn heat off, and stir occasionally as it cools. Add almond milk and refrigerate.

ALMOND - WALNUT - COCONUT MILK

Coconut cream (Tropical Traditions, page 103) combines with soaked raw walnuts and almonds to make a delicious, mellow milk. The bitterness of raw walnuts disappears in the soaking process. And the coconut cream is ready to use - just scoop out a couple of teaspoons. Walnuts are high in Omega 3's. If you can't get the coconut cream, the milk is really good with just almonds and walnuts.

1/4 cup sprouted almonds
1/4 cup soaked walnuts
2 teaspoons coconut cream
4 cups pure water

Soak walnuts in pure water for 4 - 6 hours. Drain. Combine with sprouted almonds and coconut cream, and blend as usual when making almond milk (page 40).

ABOUT KEFIR

Kefir has been around for thousands of years - maybe even longer - and its health benefits have been well documented. Kefir, a Turkish word meaning "good feeling", is a mildly fermented milk. We use kefir granules that come from the Caucasus Mountain region, where hearty folks live to be over one hundred years of age. These people attribute much of their health, stamina, and longevity to their lifestyle, and to the use of kefir and other fermented, or cultured, foods.

When Sam and Patrick were young we drank ready-made kefir - strawberry was our favorite. I noticed my stomach felt good after I drank it, but kefir was expensive, so we didn't buy it often. With four people sipping away we could finish off a quart in a single sitting and be left wanting more.

To our delight, Rex and I have discovered that we can make kefir with sprouted almond milk, reducing the cost enormously. We buy bulk almonds from Azure Standard (page 103) for about $4.00 a pound, so our cost per quart for almond milk is about 66 cents! (See page 24 for calculating how much a quart of almond milk costs.)

Rex and I are finding that kefir aids digestion, increases energy, and supports our immune systems. The friendly flora travel through the intestinal tract and "take up residence". We purchase kefir grains from Body Ecology (page 103) and they claim their kefir grains come from the Caucasus mountain region in Russia - the origin for kefir.

We drink kefir plain, add it to smoothies, seed cheese (page 63), salad dressings, put kefir in raw cookie recipes and nut balls (pages 78-79). The taste of kefir reminds me of the buttermilk I loved as a child.

Kefir works in the same way as sourdough: I save some of the first batch to make the 2nd batch. A portion of this is then used to make the 3rd batch, and so on. At the time of this writing, I've made 20 successful batches from one packet of starter grains. This makes the cost per packet insignificant. I just have to remember to save 1/2 cup for each successive batch. Otherwise a new packet of kefir grains will be opened.

With almond milk kefir I have noticed that there is separation of curds (small particles) and whey (liquid), but once gently shaken or stirred it mixes right back up. The almond-oat milk blend (following page) makes a thicker kefir that doesn't separate as much.

It is suggested to culture almond milk for 6 - 18 hours. I

think this has a lot to do with the room temperature and how warm the milk is when the fermenting begins.

When I make kefir it's usually ready in 6 hours, as I set it under the stove light (resting on a pot holder to keep the bottom of the jar insulated), where the temperature remains at about 70 degrees, even in the winter. Of course, on hot days I wouldn't need to do this.

MAKING ALMOND MILK KEFIR

3 3/4 cups almond milk made without honey (page 40)
1 packet kefir grains
1 quart wide-mouth glass jar with lid

For the first batch of kefir, pour almond milk in pan and warm to 94 degrees, or until warmth is *just begun to be felt with a finger*. I use a cooking thermometer because it is so easy to overheat. 94 degrees seems to be the perfect temperature for making kefir. Higher temperatures can weaken the culture.

While the milk is heating, I warm up the glass jar by putting some hot water into it. (This will keep the kefir from immediately cooling when it's poured into the jar.) Drain the jar before pouring in the kefir.

Remove pan from heat when it reaches 94 degrees. Add the kefir grains (or 1/2 cup from previous batch) stirring gently but thoroughly, and check the temperature again, adjusting if needed.

Pour into warmed jar. Cover immediately with lid. Set in

warm place for 4 - 6 or more hours.

When kefir has a slightly lemony, but sweet, fragrance, it is ready. Longer fermentation will give it more fizz.

I don't know how many days the kefir will remain "active" when kept in the refrigerator because we drink it up so fast! I usually make kefir a couple times a week.

Use any of the milk bends from the previous section to make delicious kefir!

ALMOND - OAT MILK KEFIR

This lovely kefir has a bit more "weight", doesn't separate as much, and has a mellow flavor. It's a good way to eat oats because the fermenting predigests the starches in the grain.

2 tablespoons uncooked quick, or baby rolled oats
1 1/2 cups pure water
1 1/2 cups almond milk (page 40)
1/2 cup kefir from previous batch,
          or, 1 packet kefir grains

Grind oats in coffee mill or blender until powdery. Put water into cooking pan, add oats, bring to a simmer. Stir over low heat until oats thicken, 2 -3 minutes. Turn heat off and cool until lukewarm. Add almond milk.

Bring almond - oat milk to 94 degrees (either by cooling more, or warming again). Then stir in one packet of kefir grains, mixing well, **or,** add 1/2 cup kefir from previous batch, checking temperature again.

Pour into warmed glass jar, cover with lid. Place under the stove light or put in a warm place to keep temperature consistent. Culture for 4 - 6 hours or longer - up to 18 hours if necessary.

Check after 4 - 6 hours to see if kefir is ready. It should smell and taste slightly lemony, and may have a slight fizz.

ALMOND MILK KEFIR SALAD DRESSING

This dressing is a bit like yoghurt salad dressing, tangy and thick. It is delicious over a bed of greens, with fresh pears on the side.

1/4 cup hulled raw sesame seeds
1/2 cup almond milk kefir
1 tablespoon favorite mustard
1/4 teaspoon yellow mustard powder (optional)

Grind sesame seeds in coffee mill or blender. Pour into bowl. Add mustard, optional mustard powder (it gives the recipe a bit more heat), and kefir, and mix by hand until creamy.

Banana Smoothie

A personal favorite for years has been the delectable banana smoothie. It's substantial enough on its own, yet when combined with other fresh fruits, or toast, makes a light meal. Serves two.

1 cup almond milk (page 40)

2 ripe organic bananas, peeled, and broken into chunks

1/4 teaspoon vanilla extract (optional)

2 - 3 tablespoons raw hemp seeds, or 1 tablespoon
    hemp seed oil for extra Omega 3's

1/2 cup optional kefir (page 50)

Pour almond milk into blender and add banana chunks, vanilla, and (optional) hemp seeds or oil. Blend for 15 seconds on low speed, then switch to high speed until bananas are thoroughly mixed. See if you can resist making a second one!

Frozen bananas work especially well for making smoothies reminiscent of ice cold milkshakes. We buy extra bananas when they are on sale and freeze them. Remove skins, break into small chunks, and store in airtight containers or freezer bags. They will last for several weeks.

FRUIT VARIATIONS

Try strawberries, dates, mangos, blueberries, peaches, or pears - or make combinations of favorite fruits. The amount of fruit will determine the thickness of the smoothie.

For additional tastes, flourishes, and flavors, try adding one of the following: cocoa or carob powder, cinnamon, allspice, clove, or nutmeg. For special occasions use fun or elegant glassware and garnish with a slice of fruit, or an extra sprinkle of spice.

KEFIR

We like to add 1/2 cup of delicious kefir (page 50) to any smoothie recipe at the end of the blending process. Reduce the amount of almond milk accordingly. The kefir adds a "hidden" flavor, extra enzymes, B vitamins, and aids digestion.

TROPICAL DELIGHT

Sipping this mouth-watering smoothie carries me away to an island paradise where I dream of white sand and turquoise water. Mangos are full of vitamins and minerals as well as betacarotene. Serves two.

1/3 cup almond milk (page 40)
1/4 cup pure cold water
1 ripe mango, peeled, and sliced off the pit
1 ripe banana, peeled, and broken into chunks
2 - 3 tablespoons coconut milk. (Freeze extra coconut
    milk in ice cube trays for later use.)
6 ice cubes

Pour almond milk, water, and coconut milk into blender. Add banana, mango, and ice cubes. Blend on low speed, then switch to high speed until thoroughly mixed. Serve immediately.

STRAWBERRY - CINNAMON SMOOTHIE

This smoothie has a luscious rosy-pink color, and a delicate, fragrant taste. Strawberries are packed with Vitamin C, and the cinnamon aids digestion. This smoothie is refreshing on a hot summer's day. Serves two.

1 cup almond milk (page 40)
1 cup fresh or frozen strawberries
2 teaspoons honey
1/2 teaspoon cinnamon powder

Rinse strawberries (if fresh), and drain excess water. Remove stems and leaves. Pour almond milk into blender. Add strawberries, honey and cinnamon. Blend on low speed, then switch to high speed until thoroughly mixed. If desired, pour through a strainer to remove seeds. Serve immediately.

TAHINI LOVER'S SMOOTHIE

I love tahini - that creamy smooth, calcium-rich, seed butter made from freshly ground or roasted sesame seeds. The tahini adds a mild, nutty flavor to the smoothie. Sometimes I grind up 2 - 3 tablespoons of raw sesame seeds in the coffee mill for a raw food version in place of roasted tahini.

Adding tahini is an easy way to stretch a small amount of almond milk when we don't have time to make up a fresh batch. Serves two.

1/2 cup almond milk (page 40)
1/2 cup pure cold water
2 ripe bananas, peeled, and broken into chunks
2 tablespoons tahini - or freshly ground sesame seeds
1 - 2 teaspoons vanilla extract

Pour almond milk and water into blender. Add bananas, tahini, and vanilla extract. Blend on low speed, then switch to high speed until thoroughly mixed. Serve immediately.

PEAR & BANANA SMOOTHIE

High fiber, cooling pears, team with organic bananas. Smooth and mellow. Strawberries make a delicious substitute for the bananas. Serves two.

1 cup almond milk (page 40)
2 ripe bananas, peeled, and broken into chunks
2 ripe pears, peeled, cored, and sliced

Put almond milk, bananas (or strawberries), and pears into blender. Blend until creamy. Serve immediately.

FIG, MANGO, & BANANA SMOOTHIE

This recipe can be made in summer when fresh fruits flood the markets, or in winter by utilizing dried fruits. Figs are said to be the highest in mineral content of all common fruits. To rehydrate dried figs, remove tough stems, cut in half, remove any bad spots, and just cover with water. Let soak for several hours, seed side down, or overnight. Soak dried mango slices for 1 - 2 hours in pure water to plump. Serves two.

1 cup almond milk (page 40)
4 fresh figs, stems removed, cut in half
    (or 4 rehydrated figs)
1/2 mango, peeled, sliced from the pit
    (or 2 - 3 large slices rehydrated)
1 ripe banana, peeled, and broken into chunks
1/2 cup kefir (page 50)

Put all ingredients in the blender and blend until smooth and creamy. Serve immediately.

BLUEBERRY - STRAWBERRY SMOOTHIE

This cooling, lavender-blue drink makes a great summer smoothie. Blueberries are high in Vitamin A and C, as well as many important minerals. Serve solo, or with a bagel or salad for a light meal. Serves two.

1 cup almond milk (page 40)
1/2 cup blueberries, fresh or frozen
1/2 cup strawberries, fresh or frozen
2 teaspoons honey (optional)

Wash blueberries and strawberries (if fresh), and remove any stems or leaves. Drain. Pour almond milk into blender, add blueberries, strawberries, and honey. Blend on low speed, then switch to high speed until thoroughly mixed. To remove excess seeds (if desired), pour through a strainer. Serve immediately.

"COCOA TALKS" HOT MORNING DRINKS

Many mornings before breakfast, Rex and I sip from hot drinks and share our dreams, goals, and ideas. We express our views about the world, explore spirituality, and share stories about "what's new".

Favorite ingredients for our cocoa talks include nutrient rich carob powder, organic cocoa powder, or teas that have spicy, full bodied flavors.

Favorite tea brands are from Celestial Seasoning: "Bengal Spice", "Roastaroma", "Madagascar Vanilla Red", or "Almond Sunset". Sometimes I like the Chai teas - Whole Foods has a blend that doesn't contain any black tea - it's just a mix of whole spices. Yogi Tea makes a delicious "Jamaican Roast" blend. Raw carob powder tastes sweeter than when roasted, but can be harder to find. Roasted carob powder has a richer, darker "base note". Azure Standard and Natural Zing are good sources (page 103) for raw carob powder. I also love Jasmine Green Tea.

A favorite soothing tummy drink includes 1/2 teaspoon organic, powdered slippery elm bark (from Mountain Rose Herbs - see index), stirred every few minutes because it thickens as it steeps.

2 - 3 teaspoons combined carob and/or cocoa powder
      or 1 tea bag per mug
3/4 cup hot water
1/4 cup almond milk (page 40)
honey, maple syrup (optional)

Bring water almost to a boil. (Boiling removes oxygen and can make the water taste flat.) Put cocoa, carob, or tea bag in mug. Add hot water. Stir. Add almond milk and sweetener. Relax, share time with someone you love, or call a friend and enjoy a special moment.

SPROUTED ALMOND SUNFLOWER SEED CHEESE

For vegans and vegetarians who miss dairy products, seed cheese delivers! It's made from sprouted sunflower seeds and almond milk or kefir. *This recipe won't taste good unless the sunflower seeds have been sprouted!* Soaking the seeds removes the strong "raw" taste and makes them sweet. The lemon and vinegar add delicious tang. This versatile recipe is adapted from the *Casa De Luz Community Cookbook: Sauces, Dressings, Condiments, and Spreads*, (www.CasadeLuz.org) given here with their blessing, and has become a staple in our diets.

There are 35 grams of protein in one cup of sunflower seeds! The look and texture of sprouted seed cheese is like ricotta or cottage cheese. We use sunflower seed cheese in any recipe that normally would call for sour cream, cheese, or yoghurt. It has found its way to roasted veggies, salads, soups, crackers, fruits, green chilies, and much more. Sprouted seed cheese is an enzyme-rich food that will last 2 - 3 days, tightly covered in the refrigerator.

Sometimes the cheese becomes a bit gray from oxidation, but this doesn't seem to affect the taste too much. The lemon juice usually keeps the cheese white and bright. Leaving the skins on the sunflower seeds makes the seed cheese grayer - taking them off makes the cheese whiter and smoother. (Method follows.)

1 cup sunflower seeds, soaked for 4 - 8 hours,
      & drained.

1/4 cup almond milk (page 40)

1 tablespoon Ume Plum Vinegar* or 1 - 2 tablespoons
      apple cider vinegar with 1/4 teaspoon sea salt

2 tablespoons freshly squeezed lemon juice

1 small clove garlic, peeled and minced (delete if mak-
      ing seed cheese to go with fruit)

additional almond milk or water to blend as needed

*Ume Plum Vinegar contains high amounts of sea salt.

Put sunflower seeds in large bowl. Cover with several inches pure water. Let soak 4 - 8 hours. Pour water off. Cover again with cool tap water. Gently rub seeds between palms of hands to remove skins, which will float to the surface.

Pour most of the water and the floating skins off. Repeat process several times. **Tip:** Pour the skins and water through a strainer to catch the few seeds that escape. These can be sorted out, or fed to the birds - they will love them!

When most of the skins are off, pour all the seeds through a strainer. Drain. Place seeds in blender or food processor with almond milk or water, lemon juice, garlic, vinegar, and salt (if apple cider vinegar is used). Blend, adding more liquid if necessary. If using a food processor, stop machine as needed to scrape down the seed cheese, and continue.

Transfer to a serving or storing container. Cover any leftovers and refrigerate for 2 - 3 days.

VARIATIONS

There are so many possible variations to try that will create flavors to enhance favorite dishes - like making a "sour cream" dip with kefir, green onions, and garlic. Use different seeds, fresh herbs or spices, and experiment - seed cheese works with most ingredients. Leftovers will last for 2 - 3 days, if covered and stored in the refrigerator

MEXICAN SPICE SEED CHEESE

1/2 cup pumpkin seeds, soaked 4 - 6 hours
1/2 cup sunflower seeds, soaked 4 - 6 hours
1/4 teaspoon chipotle powder
1 teaspoon cumin powder
1 small clove garlic, peeled, and minced
1/2 teaspoon sea salt
1/4 cup almond milk (page 40), water, or kefir (page 50)
2 tablespoons lemon juice

Pumpkin seeds add a smoky flavor which is always good with Mexican food. Soak seeds in glass container, covered with pure water. Remove skins from sunflower seeds (page 61). Pour seeds into strainer and drain. Put seeds in blender or food processor with lemon juice, spices, almond milk (water, or kefir). Blend on low speed (it works better) until seed cheese is as smooth as possible. If using a food processor, stop machine as needed to scrape down seed cheese, and continue.

Serve immediately or refrigerate for 2 - 3 days.

Fresh Herb Seed Cheese

An herbed version of seed cheese lends itself to roasted veggies, salads, soups, or dishes like lasagna.

1/2 cup cashews, soaked
1/2 cup soaked sunflower seeds
1/4 cup fresh herbs - such as basil, cilantro, rosemary
     or 1 tablespoon dried Fines Herbs blend
1 small clove garlic, peeled, and sliced
1/2 teaspoon sea salt
1/4 cup almond milk (page 40), water, or kefir (page 50)
2 tablespoons lemon juice
2 tablespoons apple cider vinegar

Soak cashews in glass container, covered with 3/4 cup water for 2 - 4 hours. Soak sunflower seeds in separate container, covered with 1 cup water for 4 - 8 hours.

Rinse and drain sunflower seeds and cashews. Remove skins from sunflower seeds as described in basic recipe (page 61), and drain. Put cashews and sunflower seeds in blender or food processor with lemon juice, spices, and almond milk (water, or kefir). Blend on low speed (it works better) until as smooth as possible. If using a food processor, stop machine as needed to scrape down seed cheese, and continue.

Sunflower Seed Cheese with Kefir

A friend of ours turned us on to this variation of sunflower seed cheese. The kefir makes the seed cheese tangy, adds even more enzymes, and tastes reminiscent of sour cream dips. Great for salad dressings.

1 cup sprouted sunflower seeds
2 - 3 tablespoons apple cider vinegar
1/2 teaspoon sea salt
1 small clove garlic
1/2 green onion finely chopped - add at very end
1/2 cup almond milk kefir (page 50)

Soak sunflower seeds for 4 - 8 hours. Remove skins as described in basic recipe (page 61). Drain off all excess water. Put sunflower seeds in blender. Add vinegar, sea salt, garlic, and kefir.

Start blender on low speed and keep at low (it actually works better than on high speed) until sunflower seeds are completely blended, about 2 minutes. Add very small amounts of kefir (a tablespoon at a time) to keep the mixture moving. If using a food processor, stop the machine to scrape down the sides as needed. Add green onions at very end.

Serve immediately, or tightly cover and keep in refrigerator. The seed cheese will last for 2 - 3 days.

SPROUTED ALMOND - CASHEW SPINACH PESTO

Imagine, an "everyday pesto" - pesto without the expense! We love to make this adapted version with spinach, cashews, and spouted almonds in place of pine nuts. A small amount of fresh basil can be added to heighten the overall flavor.

This pesto works well with all vegetables - particularly when roasted or steamed, or placed "on the side" of any green leafy salad. Making this pesto is a great way to eat lots of raw spinach and get more chlorophyll and minerals into the diet.

Spinach is extremely high in Vitamin A, and contains healthy doses of dietary fiber, Vitamin C, folate, iron, and potassium.

1 1/2 cups fresh spinach, rinsed, stems removed
1/2 cup fresh basil, rinsed, stems removed
1/2 cup raw cashews, soaked
1/8 cup sprouted almonds, skins removed (optional)
1 clove garlic, peeled and sliced
1/2 teaspoon sea salt
2 - 4 tablespoons grapeseed oil

Soak cashews, covered with 1 cup water for 2 - 4 hours. (Soaking softens the cashews.) Drain. Prepare spinach and basil, and loosely chop. Put in food processor. Add oil, salt, cashews, and almonds.

Turn on processor for about 30 seconds. Stop machine and scrape down mix from sides when necessary. Repeat process until evenly textured. (It won't get totally smooth.) This pesto tastes very nice with sliced raw veggies, or steamed/baked potatoes, with a little mustard and oil.

CILANTRO PESTO WITH SPROUTED ALMONDS & PUMPKIN SEEDS

Here's a variation of the spinach pesto recipe, but made with immune boosting pumpkin seeds and chlorophyll-rich cilantro.

1 cup rinsed, fresh spinach
1/2 cup rinsed, fresh cilantro
1/2 cup raw pumpkin seeds, soaked
1/4 cup sprouted almonds
2 - 3 tablespoons of grapeseed oil
1/4 to 1/2 teaspoon sea salt

Use leftover sprouted almonds, or start a fresh batch (page 38) Soak pumpkin seeds in glass container, covered with 1 cup pure water for 4 - 6 hours. Rinse and drain.

Cut the bottom stems off cilantro and spinach. Rinse well in cold water, shake off excess water, and loosely chop. Put in food processor. Add oil, salt, pumpkin seeds and almonds. Turn processor on for about 30 seconds. Stop machine and scrape down mix from sides when necessary. Repeat process until evenly textured. Add 1 - 2 tablespoons water if necessary to keep mixture moving (instead of using extra oil). This pesto tastes very nice with most veggies, roasted potatoes, or on a green salad.

EVERYDAY APPLESAUCE

Quick and easy to prepare, this applesauce is a wonderful way to eat an abundance of organic, raw apples. I love applesauce, but usually don't make it because of the time involved, plus the mess of clean-up. This recipe takes just 5 - 10 minutes to make (not counting optional soaking time for dates, cashews, and sunflower seeds).

Apples are an excellent source of soluble fiber, potassium, and energy. This dish makes a substantial snack or even a light meal. Serves two.

3 - 4 apples (your favorite), peeled, cored, sliced
3 Medjool dates, seeds removed, soaked 1 hour
1/2 cup raw coconut flakes
1/2 cup raw cashews, soaked 1 hour
      or 1/2 cup sunflower seeds, soaked 4 - 6 hours
1/2 cup water, or almond milk kefir (page 50)
      or plain almond milk, (page 40)

Wash apples, quarter, peel (optional), core, and slice. (Our resident crows love the peels and cores.) Put into food processor. Add dates, coconut, cashews or sunflower seeds, and water, kefir or almond milk.

Turn on machine, stopping when necessary to scrape mix down from the sides. Repeat until well mixed. Serve immediately.

RUBY RED PURIFYING SALAD
WITH SPROUTED ALMONDS

This healthful salad is packed with crunch and is bursting with nutrients, color, and flavor. Beets are known to assist the function of the liver, and to help build strong blood. Topped with sprouted almonds or sunflower seed cheese (page 61) the salad becomes a complete, light meal. Serves two, or four as a side dish.

1/2 medium beet, scrubbed, and finely grated
1 sweet apple (Fuji or Pink Lady) peeled, cored, and grated
1 large carrot, scrubbed or peeled, and grated
3/4 cup green cabbage, sliced as thinly as possible
1 tablespoon ginger root, finely grated
1/4 cup sprouted almonds, chopped, or whole

DRESSING

2 tablespoons aged rice vinegar
1 teaspoon red pepper sesame oil
1/4 teaspoon sea salt

Rinse all veggies under cold running water. In large bowl grate beet, apple, carrot, and ginger (grate extra-fine). Slice the cabbage as thinly as possible and put in bowl. Add salt and vinegar. Mix well. Drizzle with red pepper sesame oil. Toss. **Or,** *run all ingredients through a food processor.* Top with sprouted almonds (page 38), or sunflower seed cheese (page 61) and serve immediately.

Refrigerate for later use.

AVOCADO SOUP

When time is of the essence, this quick, uncooked soup
is just the right thing. Since all the ingredients are green,
the soup will be green too! But the taste is satisfying, and
the texture is smooth and creamy. Serves two.

3 cups pure cool water
1 large, or 2 medium size avocados, pit removed, peeled
    and sliced
4 - 6 stalks celery, peeled to remove strings, chopped
1 - 2 tablespoons sweet onion, chopped
1/2 large, or 1 small zucchini, chopped
1/2 cup kefir (page 50)
1 teaspoon sea salt
1 tablespoon Azuki South River Miso (or favorite
    brand) added after blending
1 green onion, or chives, minced, for garnish

Scrub zucchini and rinse onion and celery. Remove
tough strings and bad parts from celery with a knife or
vegetable peeler.

Put water, onion, avocado, celery, zucchini, kefir, and sea
salt into the blender. Blend ingredients until creamy,
adding water or kefir as needed to keep machine mixing.

Pour into bowls, sprinkle minced green onion or chives
over the top, and serve with a small dollop of favorite
miso.

GREEN POWER

When Rex and I realized we were having trouble with environmental pollution and chemical sensitivities, we learned of the rejuvenating and cleansing power of green drinks and raw food.

Trips to the health food store for daily doses of wheat grass juice helped a lot, as did making a no-nonsense green drink at home. This mind-waking, bone building, vitalizing raw food drink is packed with chlorophyll, enzymes, Omega 3's, minerals, vitamins, and amino acids! The almond milk smooths out the strong "green" taste. We would sometimes dare each other to drink this "woofie juice" (because of the reaction it would bring!) and when we did drink it, could feel powerful energy zinging into our bodies. Serves two.

1 cup pure cold water

2 cups (or more) washed raw greens. Use 2/3 milder greens such as spinach and mixed lettuces, and 1/3 stronger greens like kale, sprouts, parsley, cilantro, basil, beet tops, etc.

1 cup almond milk (page 40)

Wash greens in cold water. Drain. Chop or tear into pieces. Put in blender. Add water. Pulse to mix greens, then bend on high speed for 60 seconds. The fibers will float to the surface, and the water will be a dark emerald green. Strain liquid to collect plant fibers, pressing with a spoon. Add almond milk. Stir. Serve immediately, sipping slowly.

BUTTERNUT SQUASH BISQUE

This bisque has a gorgeous orange color, and is flavorful and warming. Butternut squash is packed with betacarotene, minerals, and vitamins. Even people who aren't crazy about squash usually enjoy this bisque. It's substantial, but not overly filling. Serve with a salad and slices of favorite whole grain bread for a complete meal. Serves four.

3 1/2 cups pure water (if making stock, following page, reduce water by 1 cup)
1 medium-large butternut squash
1 large carrot, scrubbed, and chopped
1 large potato, scrubbed, or peeled, and chopped
1 sweet apple, peeled, seeded, and chopped
1 large onion, peeled, and chopped
3 green onions, chopped
2 cloves fresh garlic, peeled, and sliced
1 bay leaf
1 teaspoon cinnamon
1 teaspoon fresh grated ginger, or 1/2 teaspoon dried ginger powder
1/8 to 1/4 teaspoon clove powder
1 teaspoon sea salt
1 cup almond milk (page 40)

Put water in a large cooking pot with lid, and place over medium heat to begin warming.

Wash vegetables. Peel if desired for stock. (Put veggie peels in a separate pan with 1 cup water. Simmer for 20 minutes. Strain. Add to large soup pot. If you make stock, reduce overall water in large pot accordingly.)

Coarsely chop carrot, potato, apple, green onions, and onion. Add veggies to cooking pot along with garlic, herbs, spices, and salt.

Cut squash in half, scrape out seeds. Put in pot with other veggies. Bring water *almost to a boil* (boiling can make the broth taste flat), and reduce heat to simmer. Cover and cook slowly until tender, about 20-30 minutes.

Remove squash halves from pot. Cool. Scoop meat from skins and put back in pot. Cool large pot for at least 10 minutes before starting to blend veggies, especially if using a glass top blender.

Make purée in several batches (or put one batch in large food processor). Pour 1/3 of veggies and broth into blender, and mix to desired consistency. Transfer to a large bowl. Repeat procedure until all vegetables are blended. Stir in almond milk. Transfer bisque back to cooking pot and briefly reheat.

If bisque is too thick, add almond milk, *a little at a time.* Adjust seasoning. Ladle into soup bowls, garnish with a sprig of fresh herbs, or a dollop of sprouted sunflower seed cheese (page 61).

Spicy Almond Quinoa

 Quinoa is a light, delicately flavored grain, and is an excellent source of vegetable protein. Quinoa contains a complete ratio of amino acids and high levels of vitamins and minerals. With a salad, quinoa makes a nutritious dinner. Couscous, or jasmine rice are tasty substitutes if quinoa isn't available. Serves three or four.

1 cup quinoa, thoroughly rinsed
1 tablespoon oil, (grapeseed, sesame, safflower)
1 medium onion, peeled, and diced
1/4 cup mushrooms, cleaned, patted dry, and sliced
2 teaspoons curry powder
3 tablespoons raw cashews
3 tablespoons seedless raisins
1 cup almond milk (page 40)
1 cup pure water
1/4 teaspoon Thai green chili paste (optional)
1/2 teaspoon sea salt

Put quinoa in a strainer and thoroughly rinse under cold running water. Check for occasional milling stones - they are light brown to dark grey in color, and about the same size as a grain of quinoa. Drain, and set aside.

In a large frying pan with lid, sauté onions in oil over

medium heat for 3 - 5 minutes. Add mushrooms, cooking
2 - 3 minutes until they soften a little. Add curry powder,
cashews, raisins, and stir quickly as spice is heated.

Add almond milk, water, Thai green chili paste, and sea
salt. Stir all ingredients until evenly distributed. Add
quinoa, bring *almost to a boil*, reduce heat to simmer. Stir
and cover.

Stir after 5 minutes, cover again, and continue to slowly
simmer for 15 minutes. When done, quinoa grains swell in
size, look translucent, smell sweet (the earthy flavor mel-
lows), become fluffy (not chewy), and will have little white
spiral "tails".

GINGER-GARLIC DIPPING SAUCE

Make while quinoa cooks.

1/4 cup reduced sodium tamari soy sauce
   or 1 - 2 tablespoons favorite miso
2 tablespoons water (increase amount with miso)
2 teaspoons honey
1 teaspoon finely grated fresh ginger root
1 clove freshly minced garlic

Mix thoroughly in a bowl. Spoon over quinoa. The sauce
will keep for several days, covered, in the refrigerator.

HAVE EXTRA SPROUTED ALMONDS?

Use whole or chopped and sprinkle on top of quinoa
before serving.

GINGER - ALMOND - TAHINI SAUCE
FOR PASTA, RICE, OR TOFU

This mildly spicy sauce is great ladled over noodles, rice, tofu, or vegetarian patties. The flavor is reminiscent of the peanutty topping that comes with cold sesame noodles from Chinese food restaurants. The tahini adds extra calcium. Serves two.

INGREDIENTS (MAKES ABOUT 2 1/2 CUPS SAUCE)

1 cup almond milk (page 40)

1 cup pure water

1 teaspoon honey

2 tablespoons tahini

1/2 teaspoon sesame hot pepper oil

4 - 5 tablespoons reduced sodium tamari soy sauce

1/2 teaspoon garam masala powder

3+ tablespoons cornstarch, or arrowroot powder

1 tablespoon grapeseed oil

3 - 4 green onions, finely sliced

Ingredients continue on following page

75

6 medium mushrooms, washed, patted dry, and sliced
4 ounce can water chestnuts, rinsed, drained, and diced
1 clove fresh garlic, minced
1 teaspoon fresh ginger, finely grated,
     or 1/4 teaspoon ginger powder

Place almond milk, water, honey, tahini, hot pepper oil, tamari, garam masala, cornstarch (or arrowroot powder), into blender and pulse until well mixed. Leave in blender and set aside.

In a large frying pan, sauté green onions, mushrooms, and water chestnuts in grapeseed oil over medium heat for 3 minutes. Add garlic and ginger. Sauté for about 30 - 60 seconds.

Pulse liquids in blender again just before pouring into pan. Stir for several minutes until sauce thickens and becomes translucent. Simmer another 1 - 2 minutes.

To adjust consistency of sauce: To thicken: Make a little batch of cornstarch with 1 - 2 teaspoons mixed with a few tablespoons of cold water. Stir this into the sauce and cook until it thickens. To thin: Add water, a few tablespoons at a time.

Jasmine, or green tea, tastes delicious with this sauce.

CLASSIC ROASTED ALMONDS

Sometimes Rex and I get a craving for roasted almonds sprinkled with sea salt, or spices such as chipotle, cayenne, chili powder, or cumin. Enjoy!

1 cup raw, unsprouted, whole almonds
1 tablespoon mild tasting oil (grapeseed, safflower)
1/4 teaspoon sea salt
1/2 teaspoon spices of choice (optional)
paper towels for draining

Heat frying pan over medium heat. Add oil and almonds. Do not let oil smoke. (Overheating oils makes trans-fats!) Turn almonds frequently with a pancake turner to avoid burning, which can happen suddenly.

Reduce heat if almonds start popping or browning too fast. (If the skins brown too quickly the inside doesn't roast completely.)

Remove almonds from pan and place on paper towels to absorb excess oil. Transfer to a plate, sprinkle with sea salt, spices, and cool (this is hard to do!). The almonds get crunchier.

Almond Milk Kefir Ginger Macaroon Raw Cookies

We make cookies in our food processor with sprouted almonds, coconut, carob powder, freshly grated ginger root, a pinch of sea salt, a little honey or maple syrup to sweeten, and a bit of kefir - just enough to hold the mix together. The ginger and kefir both add unusual flavors and aid digestion.

3/4 cup sprouted almonds
1/2 cup raw, unsweetened, coconut flakes
2 - 3 tablespoons carob powder (raw or roasted)
2 teaspoons honey, or maple syrup
2 Medjool dates, pitted and chopped into quarters
1 teaspoon fresh grated ginger root
1/4 to 1/3 cup almond milk (page 40), or kefir (page 51)

Put all dry ingredients in food processor. Blend well. Add honey or maple syrup. Slowly add almond milk or kefir through the hopper as the machine runs.

When dough starts to lump, stop motor. Transfer to a bowl to finish mixing, adding a tablespoon of kefir at a time until dough holds together, but isn't mushy.

Roll into little balls between palms (messy, but fun), put on a plate and press gently with a fork to slightly flatten. The cookies will last for several days if covered and refrigerated. Left uncovered for a few hours they dry out, making them chewier. We like them both ways.

No-Bake Almond Carob Cookies

We use leftover sprouted almonds (or sprout a new batch) for this recipe and make satisfying raw food cookies. Carob contains high amounts of calcium, iron, magnesium, copper, manganese, B vitamins, and more. Try this recipe and maybe start a new tradition!

1/2 cup sprouted almonds (page 38)
1/2 cup raw cashews
1/2 cup freshly ground sesame seeds
1/2 cup raw, unsweetened, coconut flakes, ground
1/8 cup almond milk (page 40)
3 - 4 tablespoons raw carob powder
2 teaspoons cocoa powder
2 Medjool dates, pitted and cut into quarters
1/16 teaspoon sea salt
2 teaspoons honey, or maple syrup

Rinse sprouted almonds. Grind up sesame seeds and coconut in separate batches using a blender or coffee mill. Put almonds, cashews, ground seeds, dates, carob, salt, and cocoa into food processor. Mix for about 30 seconds. Add sweetener of choice and almond milk. Mix until well blended. When dough starts to clump, transfer to a bowl. If mix is dry, add almond milk, one tablespoon at a time, because the mix can suddenly turn mushy. Work by hand (messy, but fun) until dough holds together.

Roll between palms into small balls, placing on a plate. Press balls gently with a fork to flatten. Serve with frozen banana ice cream (recipe follows).

FROZEN BANANA ICE CREAM FOR COOKIES

We make this with a Champion juicer. Ripe (*lots* of
brown spots) organic bananas make the best ice cream
and have a wonderful texture. The finished product is so
smooth and sweet it's hard to believe it's made with just
bananas.

Peel and slice **4 ripe organic bananas** (that's all!) into
1/2 inch rounds. Place on a cookie sheet and freeze for 6
hours. Remove from freezer, and run through the
Champion juicer with the "blank" attachment in place.

The ice cream comes out the Champion ready to eat.
Spoon a little on each cookie, or dish yourself up a
whole bowl and enjoy this guilt-free dessert!

BANANAS & DATES
WITH ALMOND-CASHEW CREAM

Almonds and cashews combine to make a cream that is
poured over sliced bananas and dates. We eat this
occasionally for a rich snack, sometimes with tea and
toast. For a lighter version replace the bananas and dates
with other fruits such as pears, apples, blueberries, or
mangos. Serves two.

ALMOND - CASHEW CREAM

1/4 cup sprouted almonds (page 38)
1/4 cup raw cashews, soaked 1 hour
1 cup pure cold water

1/2 teaspoon vanilla

1 teaspoon honey (if you are eating semi-sweet fruits)

Place almonds and cashews into a dry blender, and pulse as much as possible. Add water, vanilla, and honey. Blend on low speed, then switch to highest speed until smooth and velvety. Add more water for a lighter cream.

2 bananas (or other fruits)

3 - 4 Medjool dates, seeded and sliced

Slice bananas directly into individual bowls. Or prepare other fruits by rinsing, removing any stems or leaves, and putting into bowls. Top with dates, and pour the almond-cashew cream over the top.

BETTY'S GLAZED PEARS
WITH ALMOND-CASHEW CREAM
& RASPBERRY PUREE

This refreshing dessert was served at a friend's house, and it brought a rave response. The taste is delightful, and each serving is a work of art!

A raw food version can be made without baking the pears, or toasting the almonds, but prepare the other parts of the recipe before slicing the pears to keep them from turning brown. Serves four.

4 firm, but ripe pears (Bosc are good for baking)
3/4 cup *and* 1 1/2 cups apple cider or apple juice
   (used at different times, so keep separate)
1 package frozen raspberries
1/2 cup raw almonds
1/2 cup raw cashew pieces
2/3 to 1 cup pure cold water (for thickness of cream)
1 tablespoon maple syrup
1 teaspoon vanilla extract
1/2 cup toasted slivered almonds

Preheat oven to 350 degrees. Peel and cut each pear into quarters. Place in shallow baking pan and add 3/4 cup apple cider over pears. Cover with foil, and bake for 35 - 40 minutes until just tender. As pears bake, prepare the following:

RASPBERRY PUREE

Purée one package of frozen raspberries with 1-1/2 cups apple juice or cider in blender or food processor. Set aside. (The tartness of the fruit imparts a nice contrast with the other sweet ingredients.)

ALMOND-CASHEW CREAM

Pulse the nuts in blender until powdery. Add water, maple syrup, and vanilla. Blend on highest speed to get a thick cream. Adjust sweetness if needed. Chill.

TOASTED SLIVERED ALMONDS

Place almonds in lightly oiled frying pan over medium heat, stirring often for several minutes. *Watch carefully to avoid burning.* Toast until golden. Pour onto several layers of paper towels to drain excess oil. Set aside.

PRESENTATION

Place 2 - 3 tablespoons of raspberry purée on each dessert plate. Place pear quarters on purée, arranging in a fan shape. Spoon almond-cashew cream at base of pears and marbleize by slowly swirling the cream into the raspberry purée with the tip of a fork.

Sprinkle toasted almonds on top, and serve.

Porridge Nouveau

Delicious, hot cooked cereals can be made from scratch by fresh-grinding grains for 60 seconds in a blender. These cereals have exceptional flavor and are as fresh as can be! Even during the coldest days of winter, this porridge is warming and sustaining. Make with whole, organic grains whenever possible, and top with almond milk. Goldilocks never had it so good! Serves two.

2 cups pure cold water
1/2 cup whole brown rice
1/4 cup whole millet
1/4 cup rolled oats
1 tablespoon flax seeds
1 tablespoon sesame seeds
1/2 teaspoon sea salt
3 tablespoons raisins
1 cup almond milk (page 40)

Begin heating water in saucepan with a lid. Put grains and seeds into a *dry* blender and grind to consistency of corn meal - or finer if desired.

Add sea salt to water. Slowly pour in grains, stirring with a whisk or spoon. *Make sure the water isn't too hot or the porridge will clump.* Stir over high heat until cereal thickens, about 1-3 minutes, bringing *almost to a boil.* Immediately reduce heat to simmer. Add raisins. Stir. Cover and continue to simmer for 10-15 minutes, stirring occasionally.

Spoon into bowls. Serve with almond milk and a touch of maple syrup, our personal favorite.

UNCOOKED OAT GRANOLA

Uncooked, naturally sweet granola is satisfying, simple to prepare, and easy to digest. It's filling, so a little goes a long way. Oats contain minerals, vitamins and water soluble fiber.

This granola is delicious sprinkled over fresh fruit, topped with almond milk. Serves four - six.

1 cup uncooked quick rolled oats
3 - 4 Medjool dates, pitted
1 handful raisins (optional)
1/2 cup sprouted almonds or
**   other nuts or seeds**
1/4 cup raw, unsweetened
**   coconut flakes**
1/8 teaspoon sea salt
1/2 cup almond milk per
**   serving (page 40)**

Break dates into pieces. Put all ingredients in a bowl. Mix lightly. Put half of mixture into blender (or all into a large food processor) and pulse to preferred consistency.

Repeat with 2nd half and transfer to a container with lid. Refrigerate leftovers.

COCONUT - WALNUT "GRANOLA"

This "granola" is equally delicious, but is made without oats for a grain-free treat. Many people cannot digest grains, so this is a healthy alternative.

It takes just a few minutes to make, and can be eaten as is, or sprinkled over fruits, like apples, pears, figs, or bananas. Serves two - four.

1/2 cup raw, unsweetened, coconut flakes
1/2 cup raw walnuts
1/4 cup raw cashews
1/4 cup sprouted almonds
4 Medjool dates, pits removed
1/16 teaspoon sea salt
1/2 cup almond milk per serving (page 40)

Put coconut flakes, walnuts, cashews, and dates into a food processor or blender and grind until all ingredients are evenly mixed - about 30 seconds.

Spoon into bowls and top with almond milk, or sprinkle over other fruits.

FRENCH MEMORY

Ahhh - French Toast. For those of us who can no longer
eat eggs, French Toast has been a lost morning treat.
Take heart - once mastered, this recipe rivals its predeces-
sor. Some people think it's even better! The batter is a
thick almond-cashew cream that when lightly fried
becomes a toasted, flaky, nutty crust. Make with favorite
whole-grain breads for added nutrition. Too many
servings has been reported to expand waistlines! Serves
two, or three.

1/4 cup almonds (unsprouted)
1/4 cup cashews
1/2 cup, plus 2 tablespoons pure water
1 - 2 teaspoons honey
1/2 teaspoon vanilla extract
1/8 teaspoon sea salt
6 slices favorite bread
grapeseed oil as needed for frying

A note about the batter: Balancing the consistency of the batter with the heat of the pan can take a little practice. We made several attempts before getting it right, but even the bread that resembled a mangled heap still tasted incredible! Keep trying - the results are definitely worth it.

DIRECTIONS

Place almonds and cashews into dry blender and grind until as powdery as possible. Add water, vanilla, salt and honey. Blend on low speed, switching to high for about 1 minute. (The batter should be thicker than traditional whipping cream, very smooth, with little or no chunks.) Pour batter onto a dinner plate or pie dish. Set aside.

Preheat frying pan over medium heat. Dip bread into batter, but don't let it soak. Briefly allow excess to drip off. The batter should adhere well to the bread. *If it's too thick, it will cause sticking.* Thin if necessary with one tablespoon of water or almond milk at a time. *If the batter is too runny,* it won't coat the bread to make a nice crust. To thicken, put the batter back in the blender with a few more nuts, and blend for 60 seconds until smooth.

Pour oil into pan to prevent sticking. (If the oil smokes, it's too hot. Remove from heat and start over.) Place two batter-dipped slices of bread into pan. **Check for sticking after one minute** by sliding a pancake turner under the bread, adding small amounts of oil as needed. This makes turning the toast *much easier.* Cook over medium heat for about 2 - 3 minutes, until the edges turn golden.

When browned, flip bread over and cook other side for 2 - 3 minutes. Remember to **check for sticking**, adding oil as needed. *Keep a close watch because the nut crust can suddenly burn.*

Serve immediately with maple syrup, honey or jam, along with your favorite hot beverage or juice.

TEDDY BEAR PANCAKE BREAKFAST

These eggless pancakes are light and nutritious. We've had excellent results using spelt or kamut flour, ancient varieties of non-hybridized wheat, usually okay for people with wheat allergies. This recipe can be adapted to your favorite pancake mix.

EACH BATCH - 4 MEDIUM LARGE PANCAKES

When making eggless pancakes, it works best to mix up one batch at a time so the baking powder doesn't get "tired" - all those little bubbles in the batter are what make the pancakes light.

1/2 cup spelt, kamut, or whole wheat pastry flour
3/4 teaspoon Rumford's baking powder
1/3 teaspoon sea salt
1/2 cup almond milk (page 40)
oil as needed for frying (grapeseed, safflower)

Have ingredients measured and ready to go. Preheat a 12 inch heavy bottomed frying pan over medium heat. Thoroughly mix dry ingredients in bowl. Add almond milk, stirring gently until flour is absorbed. (It will swell quickly from the baking powder, so be ready to use it right away.) The batter should be "fluffy", not thick, or runny.

Pour a small amount of oil into pan to prevent sticking. (If oil smokes, the pan is too hot. Start over.) Spoon 1/4 of batter at a time into frying pan to make four medium sized pancakes.

Cook 2 - 3 minutes until little bubbles form on top of pancakes. Flip over - they should look golden brown. Cook other side for 2 - 3 minutes, adding small amounts of oil as needed.

Serve immediately, topped with maple syrup, jam, or with "Mouth-Watering Fruit Topping" (page 91).

PANCAKES
WITH APPLES & CINNAMON

Diced apples impart a delicate, fruity taste to the pancakes. Roma apples work extremely well because they cook quickly. These pancakes have fiber and taste without weighing heavily in the tummy.

Makes four medium-large pancakes.

1/2 cup spelt, kamut, or whole wheat pastry flour
3/4 teaspoon Rumford's baking powder
1/3 teaspoon sea salt
1/2 teaspoon cinnamon powder
1/2 cup almond milk (page 40)
1/4 cup apples (Roma), peeled, seeded and diced
Oil as needed for frying (grapeseed, safflower)

Have all ingredients ready to go. Prepare apples and set aside. In a bowl, mix all dry ingredients. Heat pan over medium heat. Stir apples into flour. Add almond milk, mixing gently until flour is absorbed. The batter should be "fluffy", not thick or runny.

Pour a little oil into pan. (Don't let it smoke.) Spoon batter onto pan. Cook 2 - 3 minutes on each side until golden brown. Add small amounts of oil as needed.

MOUTH-WATERING FRUIT TOPPING

This could easily become a stand-alone fruit salad (and skip the pancakes) for a lovely light breakfast! Otherwise, make the fruit topping before starting to cook the pancakes.

Uncooked version: Prepare **3 cups fruit** (blueberries, strawberries, pears, mangos, bananas, etc.). Rinse well, remove any stems and leaves. Slice strawberries. Quarter, peel, and slice pears. Peel mango, slice off the pit, and cut into smaller pieces. Sprinkle fruit with cinnamon, and sweeten if desired.

Cooked version: Prepare **3 cups fruit.** Frozen fruits are good winter choices. Place fruit in pan with a few tablespoons water. Slowly simmer for about 5 minutes. The fruit cooks down and makes its own sauce. (I add bananas at the end because I'm not fond of them cooked.) Add a sprinkle of cinnamon, and sweeten to taste with a drizzle of honey.

RICE FRITTERS

For rice lovers, this makes an hearty, irresistible pancake. Makes four medium pancakes.

1/2 cup spelt, kamut, or whole wheat pastry flour
3/4 teaspoon Rumford's baking powder
1/3 teaspoon sea salt
2/3 cup almond milk (page 40)
1/4 cup precooked rice (brown, basmati, jasmine)
Oil for frying (grapeseed, safflower)

Heat frying pan over medium heat. In a bowl, mix all dry ingredients. Pour in almond milk, stirring gently until flour is absorbed. Add cooked rice. Mix gently.

Pour oil into pan. (If oil smokes the pan is too hot. Start

over.) If batter seems too thick (it should spread out a little when placed in the pan), add almond milk, a tablespoon at a time. The batter should be "fluffy", not thick or runny.

Cook 2 - 3 minutes on each side until golden brown. Add small amounts of oil as needed.

GIANT BISCUIT

Having fun in the kitchen can bring surprises. Instead of making spoon-dropped or traditionally rolled biscuits, this recipe boasts one giant biscuit baked in a 9 inch pie plate. The first time we made the biscuit, we playfully fought over who got the last wedge! Seedless blackberry jam tastes like ambrosia with these flavors. Makes eight biscuit wedges.

3/4 cup spelt, kamut, or whole wheat pastry flour
3/4 cup oat flour - freshly ground (directions follow)
2 teaspoons Rumford's baking powder
1/2 teaspoon sea salt
1 - 1/8 cup almond milk (page 40)
1 teaspoon vanilla extract
grapeseed oil for pie dish

HOW TO MAKE OAT FLOUR

Put 3/4 cup quick, or baby rolled oats, into dry blender. Pulse for a few seconds, then switch to high speed for another 15 seconds. Voila!

Preheat oven to 375 degrees. Oil pie plate. Set aside.

Make oat flour (see previous page) in blender. Add remaining dry ingredients and pulse for several seconds to instantly mix all ingredients. Transfer to large bowl.

Add almond milk and vanilla extract. Stir until absorbed. The batter will start bubbling almost immediately.

Pour or spoon onto oiled pie dish, spreading evenly. Shake the pie plate sideways (not too hard!) a couple times to help the batter settle into place.

Put in oven. Bake until top and edges are golden brown. When done, remove from oven, cut into wedges, like pizza. Serve with seedless blackberry jam or favorite toppings.

Quick Corn Muffins

Hearty flavors of natural whole grains blend together to create a surprisingly moist corn muffin that is made without eggs, sugar, or dairy milk. Like some corn breads, this is a little crumbly. No sweetening has been added to the recipe, so feel free to top the muffins off with a little maple syrup, honey, or favorite jam. These corn muffins are delicious on their own, or with any meal. Serve with soup, salads, vegetables, smoothies, or your favorite beverages.

Corn is a high energy food and contains potassium, phosphorus, folate, and Vitamin A.

Makes 6 muffins.

1 cup fine ground yellow cornmeal
2/3 cup brown rice flour
1/3 cup spelt, kamut, or whole wheat pastry flour

1 1/2 teaspoons Rumford's baking powder
1/2 teaspoon sea salt
1 - 1/2 cups almond milk (page 40)
oil for muffin tin (grapeseed, safflower)

Preheat oven to 375 degrees. Have a 6-hole muffin tin liberally oiled and ready to go.

In a bowl, mix all dry ingredients. Add almond milk and stir gently until just absorbed. The batter will swell and become "fluffy". Make sure batter is not too thick or the muffins will be dry.

If the batter is too thick, add almond milk, a tablespoon at a time. If the batter is too runny, add a little more cornmeal, a tablespoon at a time.

Spoon batter into the muffin tin. Bake for 30 minutes (check after 20 minutes to see how muffins are doing), until the tops turn light golden brown.

Once baked, the muffins *should* easily lift out of the tin with a dinner knife. Place the muffins directly into a large serving bowl. Cover with a clean, unscented, cloth to keep them moist and warm until served.

Wrap leftovers and refrigerate.

BANANA BREAD

Much like the old favorite, this banana bread makes a lovely, not too sweet dessert or breakfast bread. The flavors mellow and improve overnight. Try toasting thick slices, topped with almond butter. Bananas are rich in potassium, and the walnuts add Omega 3 EFA. Makes one 7 inch loaf.

3/4 cup almond milk (page 40)
2 ripe bananas, peeled, and broken into chunks
1/2 cup honey
1 teaspoon vanilla extract
2 cups spelt, kamut, or whole wheat pastry flour
1/2 cup freshly ground oat flour (directions page 93)
2 teaspoons Rumford's baking powder
1 teaspoon sea salt
1/4 cup walnuts, chopped
6 - 8 walnut halves for topping
grapeseed oil for bread pan

Preheat oven to 375 degrees. Liberally oil a 7 inch bread pan to prevent sticking.

In blender or food processor, combine almond milk, bananas, honey, and vanilla. Blend on medium speed for 10 - 15 seconds.

In a bowl, mix flour, baking powder, and sea salt until well mixed. Stir in chopped walnuts.

Add liquid ingredients to dry ingredients, stirring slowly

and gently until flour is absorbed. Pour batter into the bread pan. Place 6 - 8 walnut halves (or equivalent in walnut pieces) along the top of loaf. The walnuts add extra flavor and crunch, and look beautiful on the bread.

Bake for 20 minutes. Reduce heat to 350 degrees and continue baking for 15 minutes. Check to see if it's done by inserting a toothpick into middle of loaf. If toothpick comes out clean the bread is cooked. If not, continue to bake for 5 minutes or longer. (Cover top with aluminum foil if the bread is getting too brown.) When baked to perfection, remove from oven and cool for 10 minutes.

Remove bread from pan by turning upside down onto a plate. (It *should* drop out!) Then turn right side up onto a second plate. It's easy to flip the bread over this way without it breaking. Cover bread with an unscented, clean, kitchen towel, and cool for an hour before slicing. Wrap leftovers to retain moisture and refrigerate.

GLOSSARY

Brown Rice Flour: Gluten-free flour made from whole grain brown rice. Excellent for people with wheat allergies. Comes packaged or in bulk. Available at health food stores and some supermarkets.

Garam Masala: A highly aromatic blend of Middle Eastern spices, available in Asian food sections at supermarkets and health food stores.

Kamut Flour: A rediscovered ancient non-hybridized form of wheat, grown since the times of Egypt. It rates 20-40% higher in protein than modern, cultivated varieties. Most people with wheat allergies can eat kamut. Comes packaged or in bulk. Available at health food stores.

Millet: A golden round grain, high in protein, and easy to digest. It has a combined sweet and bitter taste. We prefer it mixed with other grains. Available bulk or packaged at health food stores.

Quinoa: An ancient grain grown in the Andes Mountains in South America. Quinoa contains the highest amount of protein of any grain, supplying all eight essential amino acids in balance. Available packaged or in bulk at health food stores and supermarkets.

Rumford's Baking Powder: Many brands of baking powder are made with aluminum. Studies have linked high levels of aluminum in the body with Alzheimer's Disease. Aluminum pots and pans may also be an issue.

Rumford's Baking Powder is aluminum free, and works just as well as other brands. Available at all supermarkets and health food stores.

Sea Salt: Sea salt is a natural, sun dried salt containing vital trace elements and minerals. There are many varieties such as Celtic, Dead Sea, French, all with subtle flavors and concentrations of minerals.

Regular table salt is subjected to extremely high processing temperatures, and contains additives to make the salt pour easily. Sea salt is available bulk or boxed in supermarkets and health foods stores.

Spelt Flour: Recently rediscovered, this nearly lost grain - an early form of wheat - was grown on a few mountainside farms in the Alps. Spelt is good for most people with wheat allergies and has a delicious, delicate flavor. Available in bulk or packaged at health food stores.

Tahini: A creamy smooth, golden seed butter made from roasted or raw sesame seeds. Available in jars or tins at supermarkets and health food stores.

Thai Green Chili Paste: Very hot and spicy! A little goes a long way, and adds delicious, full bodied, aromatic flavor. Comes in little jars. Available in the Asian food section at supermarkets.

REFERENCES

Ann Wigmore, *The Sprouting Book*. Avery Publishing Group.

Viktoras Kulvinskas, M.S., *Survival into the 21st Century*. 21st Century Publications.

Nutrition Almanac. McGraw Hill.

Historical and botanical information adapted from: Draft 5, *The History of Almonds*, Dale E. Kester, Professor Emeritus, Pomology Department of the University of California at Davis, July 1991.

"A Treasury of Western Nuts", Jerry Anne De Vecchio, *Sunset*, November 1966.

"4 Forbidden Treats that Help Your Health: Nuts Lead to Longer Life", Barbara Tunick, *Womans World*, June 1997.

"Vitamin E Against Heart Disease", *Food Product Design*, July 1966.

"Don't Knock Nuts—Inside the Shell are Nuggets of Nutrition", Meghan E. Flynn, M.S., R.D. *Environmental Nutrition*, April 1997.

"Nuts to Everybody!", *Food Processing*, December 1996.

"U.S. Promotes Health Nuts", Ela Schwartz, *American Food and Ag Exporter Directory*, Winter 1996.

"Eat and Run", Sarah Belk King, *Sports Traveler*, Spring 1996.

"Good News in a Nutshell", Peter Jaret, *Health*, July/August 1996.

"Nuts to You", *UC Berkeley Wellness Letter*, February 1997.

"Health Nuts", Kimbra Postlewaite, *Snack Food*, July

1996.

"Foods that Make You Look and Feel Better", Joan Wilen and Lydia Wilen, *Parade*, November 1996.

"Nuts for Nutrition", Marie Simmons, *Bon Appetit*, June 1996.

"Nuts: Good and Good for You", Bill Lacey, *Culinary Review*, November 1996.

"Mother Nature's Little Helpers", Colleen Dunn Bates, *Cooking Light.*

"A Healthy Nut", Fran LaBell, *Prepared Foods*, July 1997.

"Nuts—A Healthful Choice", *The American Dietetic Association*, 1997.

"Almonds, Naturally", *The Almond Board of California.*

"Nuts and Nutrition", *PMK Associates, Inc.*, 1995.

"Odwalla Bottles New Drink", Associated Press, *Modesto Bee*, May 1997.

"Drink Your Meal", *San Francisco Chronicle*, May 1997.

"6 Secret Disease-Fighters", Jean Carper, *Eat Smart*, January/February 1997.

"Rice Flour Makes Its Mark", Sandy Parlin, *Food Processing*, October 1997.

"Foods of Tomorrow", *Food Processing*, October 1997.

"Milk: Does It Do A Body Good?", Anthony J. Cichoke, MA, DC, DACBN, *Energy Times*, January/February 1995.

Mail Order Resources

Azure Standard: our favorite for quality and pricing
79709 Dufur Valley Road
Dufur, OR 97021
541-467-2230
www.azurestandard.com

Natural Zing
www.naturalzing.com

Mountain Rose Herbs
www.mountainroseherbs.com

Body Ecology (kefir starter)
www.bodyecologydiet.com

South River Miso: Many varieties, including soy-free
www.southrivermiso.com

Tropical Traditions
www.tropicaltraditions.com

**The Almond Board of California
(for information on almonds)**
www.almondsarein.com (consumer site)

Favorite Raw Food Books

Living On Live Food, by Alissa Cohen.
Her DVD (same title) is a wonderful resource if you are
interested in learning how to make raw food.

Raw, The Uncook Book, by Juliano

Hooked on Raw, by Rhio

The Sprouting Book, by Ann Wigmore

Warming Up To Living Foods, by Elysa Markowitz

FAVORITE RAW FOOD WEBSITES

Alissa Cohen - The Living And Raw Food Diet
www.alissacohen.com

The Garden Diet (Ekaya Institute) - great email newsletter
www.thegardendiet.com

Shazzie - Loving And Living A Beautiful Life In The Raw
www.shazzie.com

Woody Harrelson and Laura Louie's Voice Yourself
www.voiceyourself.com

FAVORITE VEGETARIAN COOKBOOKS

Vegetable Heaven, by Mollie Katzen

Rebar Modern Food Cookbook, by Audrey Alsterbery and Wanda Urbanowicz. This isn't a "pure" vegetarian cookbook (there are a few fish recipes), but it is loaded with creative cooking ideas.

VEGAN & VEGETARIAN WEB SITES

Vegetarian Times
www.vegetariantimes.com

International Vegetarian Union
www.ivu.org

North American Vegetarian Society
www.navs-online.org

The Vegetarian Resource Group
www.vrg.org

Please feel free to contact me with questions
or comments through the Almond Essence website:

www.almondessence.com

ACKNOWLEDGMENTS

To our parents, family members, and the many dear people whose excitement, encouragement, recipe testing, and input helped to make this book a reality, we extend our deepest gratitude.

Most especially to our sons, Patrick and Sam, for their spirited contributions, and to the special women their lives, Ruth and Sarah, we thank you wholeheartedly.

To our friends Rose & David Alpert, Jane Cunha, Bruce Manly, Jim & Betty Dew, Becca & Kurt Anderson, Susan Russo, Fred & Mary Vogt, Laurie & Walt Zabel, Dr. Jeffrey Klass and Raine, Jody Pinilla, Jim O'Dea, Dorothy Martin Neville, Linda & Harry Stanbridge, Sarah Wachenheim, Penny Kent, Penny Hill - you all encouraged me at just the right moment to continue with this project.

For suggestions and inspirational support in the early stages, thanks to Mary Carroll Moore. For sensitive teaching methods and insightful editing, recognition and heartfelt thanks to Dick Ridington. We are grateful to Heidi Savage at the Almond Board of California while researching the book for her assistance and encouragement.

To Kathleen & Gerald Hill, Linus Mauer & Mary-Jo Starsiak for direction and laughter. To Linda Miller, Joan Foberg, Terrie Lambert, and Rhonda Stapleton, for enthusiastic responses, encouragement to "keep the faith", and insightful viewpoints that helped me to "make it so!"

And to Lillian Harvey for joining me in the adventure of making almond milk and raw food recipes with dedicated spirit and love.

May The Blessings Be!

CPSIA information can be obtained at www.ICGtesting.com
Printed in the USA
BVOW030506170113

310755BV00001B/146/A